Interdependence of Living Things

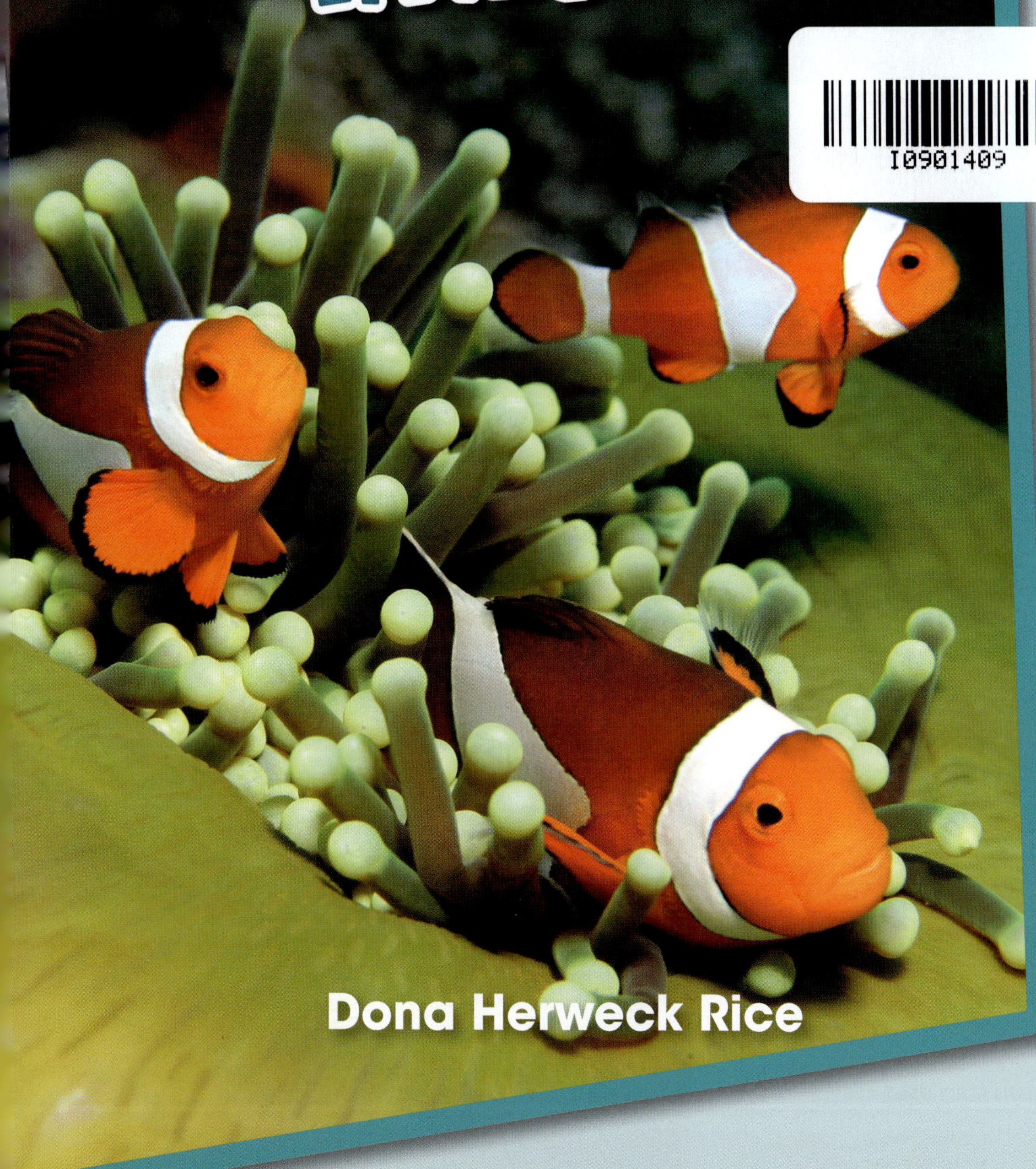

Dona Herweck Rice

Consultants

Sally Creel, Ed.D.
Curriculum Consultant

Leann Iacuone, M.A.T., NBCT, ATC
Riverside Unified School District

Image Credits: pp.12–13 Anthony Pierce/Alamy; p.10–11 iStock; p.12 top) Getty Images; p.26 Frances M. Roberts/Newscom; p.8 (top) Medical Stock Photo/ Newscom; p.27 Peter Bennett/Ambient Images/ Newscom; p.25 (top) Reuters/Newscom; pp.28–29 (illustrations) Janelle Bell-Martin; all other images from Shutterstock.

Library of Congress Cataloging-in-Publication Data

Rice, Dona, author.
Interdependence of living things / Dona Herweck Rice ; consultant, Sally Creel, Ed.D., curriculum consultant, Leann Iacuone, M.A.T., NBCT, ATC Riverside Unified School District, Jill Tobin, California Teacher of the Year semi-finalist Burbank Unified School District.
pages cm
Summary: "All living things need one another to survive. Each living thing gives something to Earth and has its own special needs. Working together keeps the circle of life going."— Provided by publisher.
Audience: K to grade 3.
Includes index.
ISBN 978-1-4807-4599-5 (pbk.)
ISBN 978-1-4807-5066-1 (ebook)
1. Ecology—Juvenile literature.
2. Biotic communities—Juvenile literature.
3. Food chains (Ecology)—Juvenile literature. I. Title.
QH541.14.R485 2015
577—dc23

2014014105

Teacher Created Materials
5301 Oceanus Drive
Huntington Beach, CA 92649-1030
http://www.tcmpub.com

ISBN 978-1-4807-4599-5

Printed by: 590835
Printed in: Taiwan

Table of Contents

Interdependence

It's a big word! *Interdependence*. What does it mean? Let's break it down.

Inter- is a prefix, or word beginning. It means "between or together." Knowing what a prefix means helps you know what the word means.

Inter-

Since you know what *inter-* means, can you figure out what these words mean?

- interrupt
- interview

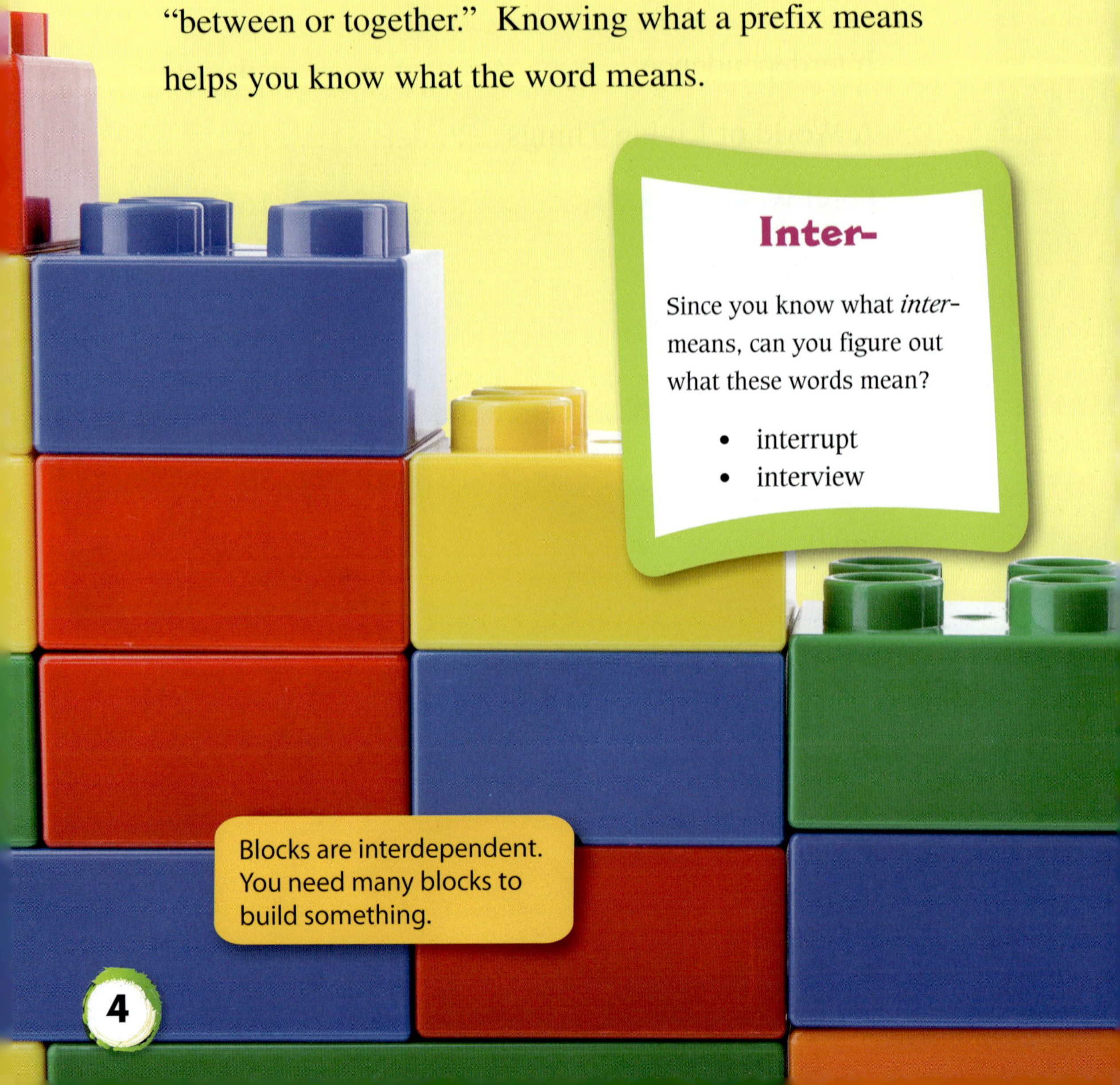

Blocks are interdependent. You need many blocks to build something.

Depend means "to rely or count on." *-Ence* is a suffix, or word ending. It means "a state or condition."

Put them together! *Interdependence* means "a state in which two or more things rely on each other."

These logs are interdependent. Each log needs the other logs for the house to stand.

The world is filled with interdependence! No living thing **survives** on its own. Living things depend on many other things to survive.

Nonliving things do not need other things. But nonliving and living things **affect** them. They are changed by what is around them. Living and nonliving things are connected in many ways!

In-

In- is a prefix that means "not." So *independence* means "the state of *not* relying on anything else."

Water is a nonliving thing. But all living things need water.

A World of Living Things

Life is everywhere on Earth! Wherever you go, you will find it. You may not see it, but it is there. Whether plant, animal, or **bacteria** (bak-TEER-ee-uh), living things are all around you.

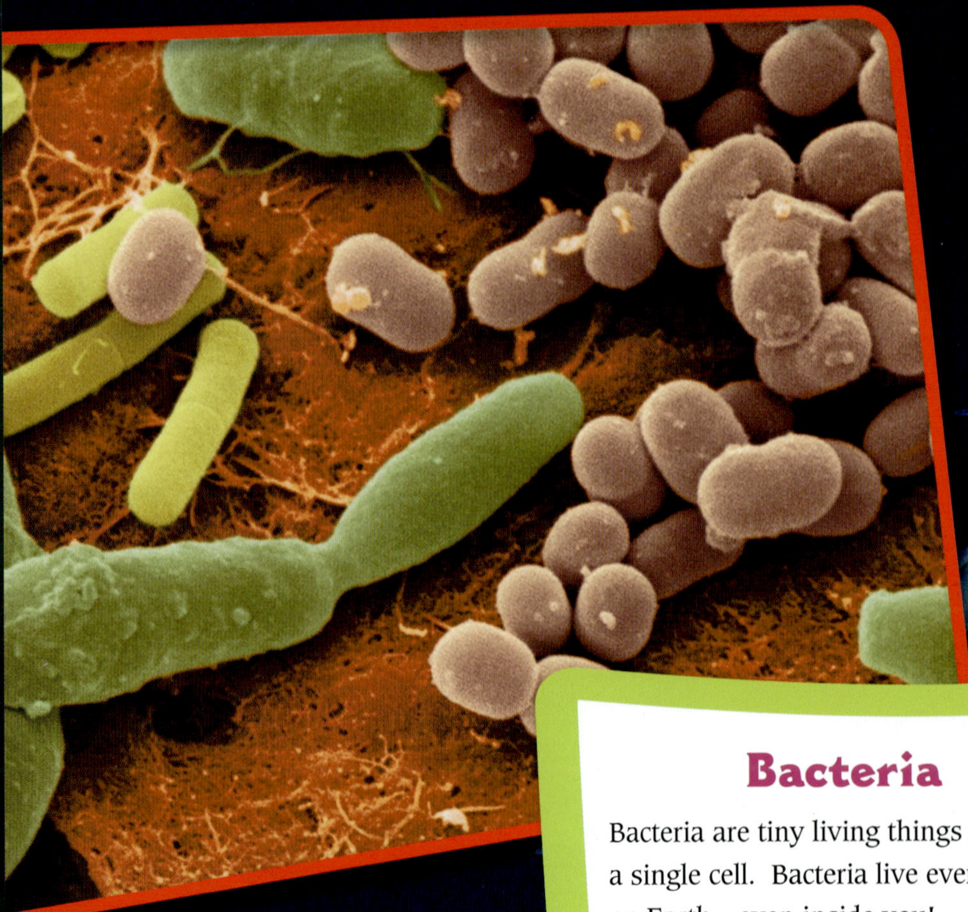

Bacteria

Bacteria are tiny living things made of a single cell. Bacteria live everywhere on Earth—even inside you!

Are you traveling through the ocean? You will find living things there. They are everywhere, down to the deepest depths. Are you traveling through the sky? You will find living things there. They are everywhere, for miles up into the clouds. You will find life whether you travel to the freezing poles or to the driest deserts. The world is full of living things!

Living things can be found in many places.

And that's not all. Each of these living things is connected in some way. What one living thing does will have an **effect** on other living things. Some effects are so small that you would never see them. Some are huge and life-changing. But nothing, no matter how small, happens without affecting something else.

The spider finds its prey.

Think of a spider web. The spider builds the web by weaving all the threads together. If a bug lands on the web, it affects all the threads. No matter where the spider is on the web, it knows its next meal will be there. Living things are like this. One small change affects many other things.

Tiny but Mighty

Think of the tiny krill that are found in Earth's oceans. Each krill is only about as long as your thumb. But krill are food for many kinds of sea life. What if a new **disease** affected the krill? They would start to die out. What would that mean for other sea life? Animals as big as whales eat krill. If there were no krill, many animals would be affected. Some sea animals would not have enough food to eat. They may die. What would that mean for us?

Krill are shrimp-like animals that live in the ocean.

These humpback whales eat krill.

The Buzz

Right now, a small insect is in big trouble. This insect is very important to us all. The insect is the honeybee. Many plants depend on it. And many animals depend on plants. We do, too!

Many honeybees are getting sick and dying. And we are not sure why! **Chemicals** (KEM-i-kuhlz) may be the problem. An insect called a *mite* may be the problem. But no matter what, the bees are going away.

Mites may be causing bees to die.

Bees carry and move the pollen that most plants need to grow new plants. The plants depend on the bees. They could not survive without them. Do small things matter? You can *bee* sure they do!

Food Webs

One of the best ways to see interdependence is in a food web. Food webs show how energy is passed between living things.

A caterpillar eats a leaf.

All energy comes from the sun. The sun's energy helps plants grow. Animals eat the plants. Some animals eat other animals. Animals die, and their bodies **nourish** the soil. Plants use the soil to grow. And so on and so on. This is what some people call the *circle of life*.

Everything in a food web depends on other things. If any part is gone, the other things in the web must **adapt**. If they cannot, they may die.

The food web on this page shows how living things work together. The arrows show the direction the energy flows. Everything in this web depends on one another.

Humans

Humans are a part of many food webs. How do you think humans fit in?

energy
energy
energy
energy
nergy
energy
energy
energy

Ecosystems

Food webs are part of **ecosystems**. Ecosystems are found throughout the world. An ecosystem is a group of things that live together. It is made of living and nonliving things. They work together to survive. They need one another.

Three Types

There are three main types of ecosystems: marine (saltwater), terrestrial (land), and freshwater.

terrestrial ecosystem

Each ecosystem is unlike any other. It has its own types of land, water, and weather. It has its own types of plants and animals. Any change would make it a new ecosystem.

marine ecosystem

freshwater ecosystem

What is found in an ecosystem has a lot to do with its **environment**. The environment is what is around something. Air and water are part of it. So is land. Living and nonliving things are, too.

The environment supports the ecosystem. A hot and **humid** one may support a rainforest. A mild one may support a grassland. A cold one may support a forest. A dry one may support a desert.

A healthy ecosystem is in balance. Too much or too little of any one thing is bad. It is just like the story of *Goldilocks and the Three Bears*. Everything has to be just right!

Something may happen in nature to change its balance. A flood or fire may harm things. The rain may stop. The weather may grow colder or hotter.

People may destroy nature, too. We may cut down too many trees. We may pollute the water, air, or land. We may harm a type of animal or its home.

We may change an ecosystem forever. It may never be the same. But remember—we are all connected. What we change also changes us. What we damage also damages us. We are many pieces of a puzzle. But we are also one big picture.

Pollution can hurt or kill plants and animals.

Independence

As each of us grows up, we learn to take care of ourselves. We work to earn money. We cook and eat food. We shop for what we need. We try to do it on our own.

But no matter how hard we try, we cannot do it alone. We are never *really* independent. We depend on plants and animals for food. We depend on the air, the sun, and water to live. We depend on other people at school and work. We need other people to share with and love. We need to take care of our world and be good to one another. Our own health depends on it!

HERB PROJECT

Let's Do Science!

How are the parts of an ecosystem related? See for yourself!

What to Get

- blocks
- book or website about an ecosystem
- marker
- masking tape

What to Do

1. Read about an ecosystem and the living and nonliving things found there.

2. Write the name of each living and nonliving thing on pieces of tape. Attach the tape to blocks. The blocks will stand for those things. If there is a lot of something, label more blocks. If there is a little, label fewer blocks.

3. Stack the blocks in a tower. The things that there are more of should be on the bottom. The things that there are fewer of should be on top. (The floor can be the sun.)

4. What happens if you pull out one block or more? What does the tower show you about ecosystems?

Glossary

adapt—to change to deal with new conditions

affect—to cause change

bacteria—single-celled living things

chemicals—substances made from chemical processes

disease—an illness

ecosystems—everything that exists in certain places

effect—a change that results when something is done or happens

environment—surroundings

humid—having a lot of moisture in the air

nourish—to provide with food

survives—remains alive

Index

Your Turn!

Web Watching

Look for a spider web, either indoors or outdoors. How is it made? Are the threads interdependent? Try to make a web out of string or pipe cleaners. When you touch one thread, what happens to the others?